MW01124720

The Unce~~nsored Mafia~~
Guide for College Students.

Essential Advice for Surviving College and Dorm Life.

Everything I Wish I Knew Before School

by
Antonio Rossini

Copyright: Antonio Rossini

Published: July 14 2015

Disclaimer:

The information in this guide book is provided and sold with the knowledge that the publisher and author do not offer any legal or other professional advice. In the case of a need for any such expertise, consult with the appropriate professional. This book does not contain all information available on the subject. This book has not been created to be specific to any individual's or organizations' situation or needs. Every effort has been made to make this book as accurate as possible. However, there may be typographical and or content errors. Therefore, this book should serve only as a general guide and not as the ultimate source of subject information. This book contains information that might be dated and is intended only to educate and entertain. The author and publisher shall have no liability or responsibility to any person or entity regarding any loss or damage incurred, or alleged to have incurred, directly or indirectly, by the information contained in this book. You hereby agree to be bound by this disclaimer or to not read this book.

Table of Contents

Introduction

For years I've been giving the advice in this book to my nieces and nephews before they go to college. I can't tell you how many phone calls and thank you notes I've received because of it. We have a big family. This year my nephew, Angelo said, "Uncle Antonio, your advice is great. Why don't you write a book?"

There are four ways to learn things: trial and error, in school, on the street, and from people who have been there, done that.

I feel compelled to share with the kids already in college, and those on their way, the things that can mean the difference between a happy and a hellish college life. Not everything in this book would be considered moral or ethical. I hate injustice and I hate the rats in this world, rude roommates, bad teachers, unfair officials and scumbags that take advantage of young people. I hate seeing good people get screwed. This book lays out in simple terms the things every college kid should know that you won't find in a school hand book.

For this book I've interviewed all of the family member graduates in: Engineering, Business, Teaching, Nursing, Computer Science, Communications, Biology and Art. I asked them, "What do you wish you had known before college? What tips do you have for kids that aren't found in the school handbook? What helped you get through school?" The answers may surprise you.

There's more than one way to paint a house. You may or may not agree with everything in this book. If you don't, that's fine. Some of you may find something in this book too timid, while others may see the same thing as extreme. Use common sense.

The stories in this book are true and the advice offered has been used. That's not to say you should take it. See the preceding disclaimer.

Let me say that neither my family nor I are in the mafia or have ever been in the mafia. I do not condone criminal activity. (See Chapter 4: DENY EVERYTHING)

Chapter 1
On Teachers

Get the best teachers:

This piece of advice can make the difference between a great school year and one mixed with pain and suffering every waking minute. Get the best teachers. This isn't always possible freshman year. To get the best teachers, teachers you're most likely to get the best grades from with minimal effort, you need to talk to upperclassmen who share your major and to ask them, "Who should I take whatever class 101 with?"

It's important to be specific of the subjects you're taking so you get the best information. I've had upperclassmen tell me, "Don't get professor so and so, whatever you do!"

I was once told, "Get partial credit Crawford for calculus." And that upperclassman was right on the money. Professor Crawford would give tons of partial credit for answers or formulas that were correct up to a certain point.

In thermodynamics I received an F along with the rest of my class. That's right, my whole class failed. The professor was a bit screwed up; his wife had worked in the chemistry department before an experiment explosion took her life. The second time I took thermodynamics with another professor I got an A- and actually enjoyed the class.

Sit up front:

When you sit in the classroom always tried to sit as close to the front as possible and to the left hand side, the student's left, the professor's right. This is the place in the room where the professor will most naturally look. It is also the place in the room where the students get the highest grades. If you sit in the back of the classroom or lecture hall you may as well not bother going, as you will surely fail. Class time is solo time not social time.

In my chemistry 101 class, at the start of term, the

lecture hall was filled with 300 students. At the end of the semester 40 of us were left. Don't use other students as your barometer or measuring device to see how well you are doing in school. Colleges let in far more students than they graduate. Where I went to school there was a 60% failure rate in engineering. I believe it was actually higher since my freshman classes were huge and my senior classes were quite small, ranging in size between a dozen to two dozen students.

Bailing is not quitting. It's smart:

Many people stay in miserable situations because they're afraid of being a quitter. They'll stay with rotten boyfriends or girlfriends or at a rotten job. Some people think that if they do this they're being strong. I think they're being stupid.

My brother took an English class on female authors. It turned out to be a class in feminism under a different name. After the first test the students compared results and, mysteriously, all the boys had very low grades while all the girls had high grades. My brother didn't see this boding well for his GPA and, in my opinion, made the right move to withdraw from the class. It's not a crime to bail on a class that's being taught by a bad, sexist, racist, chauvinistic or jerky teacher. It's not quitting.

I had a chemistry teacher who called in several other teachers to gawk at a girl who was very short and had to use a box to stand on to do her chemistry experiments. The girl was so embarrassed she dropped out of school. I wish her parents had made a big deal out of it. Bullies stink. It's important to check schools out before you go. Talk to students in attendance that are taking your major to see how they like the school and the teachers. A lot of schools have buildings dedicated to different fields such as business, art and engineering. Look at the faces of the students. Do they look totally stressed out? If so, it might be time to look at other schools.

Summer classes are easy:

Teachers are human; they can be many things: they can be kind and helpful or, like most humans, they can be power-hungry. Like store clerks who have no business standing behind the counter, to some teachers a student's presence is no more than an irritation. I have known professors who will fail an entire class of students. I had a professor who, at the start of the term said, "If you need any help you can always find me in my office."

It came as a shock when I knocked on his door and he told me he had no time for me. His mantra to the class was "You people have to do some serious soul-searching." whatever that was supposed to mean. If you find you have a professor who is causing you grief, one who will take your time away from all your other classes as well as bring down your grade point average you have several options: you can withdraw from the class and take it the next time it is offered with another professor or, what I liked to do, take the class during the summer. Summer classes, I found, are always quite a bit easier than those during the regular school year. I took one that met once a week for four hours. No teacher likes to teach for four hours straight. After 2 1/2 hours the teacher would always say, "Why don't you all head to the beach." and that's exactly what I did.

The hardest class you will ever take:

I walked into an electromagnetic theory class and sat down. The student next to me asked, "How many times is this for you?"

I replied, "Times for what?"

He said, "This is my third time taking this class."

That made me somewhat apprehensive but not nearly as much as when the professor said maliciously, "Welcome to the hardest class you will ever take in this university."

I immediately stood and walked down towards his podium with a pink withdrawal slip. I placed it on the podium and said, "Please withdraw me from this class."

The teacher, with a look of surprise asked, "Why?"

I said, "I would be a fool to stay in this class after what you just said."

He signed the slip withdrawing me and I took electromagnetic theory over the summer and got a B.

Use your teachers:

If you see a professor off campus or pass one in the hall be sure to say hi and to use their name, "Hi Professor So and so." Teachers, like all humans, like to be acknowledged.

When a semester is over and you find you have a good grade from a professor, go to their office and say thank you for your excellent teaching. You may need them as a reference or contact in the future.

Chapter 2
On Roommates

Set rules up front:

Headphones are great! At start of term I came into my room and found that my new roommate, who I had yet to meet, had a heavy metal bumper sticker on his desk as well as a big stereo. It surprised him somewhat when we first met when I said, "Hey, you have a big stereo and I have a big stereo. Let's go to the mall and pick up some headphones. He looked a little taken aback but went nevertheless. I got to listen to my music in peace while he got to listen to his heavy metal. Occasionally he would drum some pencils on his desk and scream out a lyric, but that I could deal with.

Set rules upfront with your roommate such as times when boyfriends or girlfriends come to visit or stay over. Set boundaries like: what's mine is mine and don't touch my stuff. Never give anyone carte blanche. If your roommate does things that you do not like, talk to your roommate. Don't gossip! If you have nothing good to say about someone, don't say it. Also, don't tell people negative things about yourself including your roommate. Anything negative you say about yourself, your past or your family can and will be used against you. Never take it for granted that anyone will keep your secrets. Remember, you will be spending years in your college. If you have skeletons in your closet, don't be too quick to open the door and show them to people. If you find other students gossiping or dragging someone through the mud don't be too quick to chime in. I remember when, one day, my suitemates (there were 10 of us per suite) were all hanging out on my roommate's side of the room. A new student was due to move in and had left their clothes and books in their room. One of my fellow suite mates said, "Let's make the new guy's life hell." The others, like a pack of jackals, quickly chimed in with, "Yeah!" and "Absolutely!" I looked on in stunned disbelief until one of my suitemates noticed my silence and asked, "What do you think?" I stood up and walked over to the person and said, "I'll tell you what I think!" I went from one suite mate to the next saying, "I think that you're going to be nice to him! And if you're not, you'll answer to me!" I hate fighting but I hate bullies more. I was incensed that people could be gunning for a kid they'd never met.

Don't be a bully. Years from now, after college, you don't want to have to live with the regret of having been a bully.

My roommate was a drug dealer:

At one point I lived off campus and didn't like it very much. By the way, if you're over 18 your parents do not have to sign any rental or lease agreement for where you live. It's against the law. If the people you live with decide to have a crazy party and the house is totally trashed, you don't want your parents to get sued for the damage. Anyway, I decided to move back into the dorms. My new roommate ended up being a drug dealer. I realized this when he would get phone calls and would be pleading into the phone, "I'll get you the money, man! I'll get you the money!" Needless to say, I slept with my wallet under my pillow and kept my more valued possessions with my friends in their rooms. Finally, after my roommate had burned half the incense in China to cover up the smell of his drugs, I decided I had had enough. I went down to the housing office and asked for a new room. I was told, "We have no open rooms." The woman said it with a grin, which ticked me off, and I decided to make it my quest. I replied to her, "I'll find a room."

I walked through the dorms asking people I knew and people I didn't know if they knew anyone who needed a roommate. One guy spoke up and said, "There's a guy in my suite whose roommate didn't come back this year."

15 minutes later I met that guy, who seemed like he was pretty cool. I went down to housing and a few days later I moved in with my new roommate. There's an old adage: when a door closes another opens up.

Everyone has a boss:

Don't give up when you need something. Everyone has a boss. I received a letter saying that my scholarship was declined and on top of that a letter that said that I had to move out of the dorms for the insufficient funds. I went down to the housing office where the woman behind the desk told me, "Then you have to move out."

I told her that I didn't have anywhere else to go and she said, "That's too bad."

Directly behind this woman's desk was a hallway with brass plaques on the doors. I walked quickly around her desk and headed for the door with the largest brass plaque. Not bothering to knock, I opened the door and walked in, followed by the crabby woman who was yelling, "I told him not to come in here! I told him not to come in here!"

A portly, balding man was sitting behind the desk. He looked up from his papers and asked, "What's going on here?" I told him about the letter and he dismissed the crabby woman. He said, "Don't worry." It turned out that he was the Director of Housing. He told me, " Go to the financial office and tell them you need an emergency loan, and in the meantime, you don't have to move out."

I did as he asked and got an emergency loan to cover my scholarship. Everyone has a boss and I found the crabby woman's boss. Just because someone says something doesn't make it true. There's always help when you need it

Upperclassmen aren't Gods:

Remember that nobody is more important than you. If an upperclassman tells you that you're not allowed to do something at a certain time you can say one of the most powerful words in the English language: NO!

On my first day in the dorm two seniors said to me, "Don't go in the bathroom between eight and nine, that is our time. Don't go in the kitchen between such and such and such and such, etc." I looked the two seniors in the eye, who, incidentally were much bigger than I, and said, "You're talking to the wrong guy." The seniors turned around without another word and walked away. Most people who act tough aren't. If you make the decision that you are not going to be bullied early on it makes life a lot easier. Usually a simple statement of fact such as, "That ain't gonna happen." Is more than enough to deter a bully.

Roommates come in all different shapes, sizes and temperaments. You don't have to "like" your roommate to get along with them. Ground rules and mutual respect are the foundation for a healthy roommate relationship.

If you're living off campus meet your roommates before signing anything. Ask them questions about their party habits as well as questions to gauge their mental health.

Make sure there's a fire escape. I once lived in an attic that was hot as bloody hell in the summer, next to a fire station and on the corner of a busy intersection. The only good thing about that place was the French exchange student.

Nerd Bullies:

One type of bully that I hate is the "nerd Bully". Nerd bullies pick on people who don't look or talk like the stereotypical nerd. They ostracize the non-nerd from study groups and discussions in an effort to keep them from learning. Since they're "nerds" and most often taken to be the victims of bullies, they're not often taken to task for their bullying. Nerd bullies suck.

Chapter 3
There's Always Help

If you get behind in your studies or you feel really depressed there's always help. It might just take a little time to find it. One day I was feeling pretty bummed out and I happened to say to one of my friends, "Hey, I'm kind of bummed out. Do you have a few minutes to talk?" I had never asked anyone that in my life and I was shocked and annoyed when my friend answered "no." Being of an inquisitive mind, I made an experiment of it by going to other friends and saying, "Hey, I'm kind of bummed out. Do you have a minute to talk?" One after another all my "friends" said no. Feeling ticked off, I turned to people I didn't know to see what they would say. Well, there's this one guy who, I thought, was pretty stuck on himself and I didn't like him very much. I asked him if he had a minute to talk and he surprised me by not only saying yes, he invited me into his room set me at his desk and offered me a soda. He sat on his bed and asked, "What would you like to talk about?"

I told him, "You are the only one that would take the time to talk to me."

He was gratified to hear it and asked me, "So, do you want to talk?"

I said, "No. I'm cool. You restored my faith in human nature."

If you need someone to talk to and can't find someone right away keep looking. There is also a student resources office in most colleges, and lots of hotlines a person can call as well. I'm not saying that I was at the end of my rope, but my "friends" lack of compassion made me feel concerned for anyone who is.

On extra help:

Prerequisites are important. If you find that you're lacking information for any subject, you need to do something about it. Most colleges have a place where they keep their tutors. My geometry skills were pretty much nonexistent when I started taking calculus. I would go to the tutors every day to learn geometry. Without the tutors I don't believe I ever would have graduated. I also would go to the campus bookstore to get supplements for each of my classes. For example: When I was studying optics and lasers I found a wonderful book with example questions and answers and detailed step-by-step instructions for the problems. This supplement helped me greatly. The optics and lasers teacher also posted solutions to homework in the library and I made it a point to double check mine regularly. I found that in one of my classes a lot of the students were having a hard time so I started a study group in the afternoons where we could all meet and go over homework problems and prepare for tests. The six of us in the group were the only people that passed the class. Please note that this was a particularly tough class with a particularly tough professor. This was by no means the norm.

Chapter 4
Deny Everything

I wasn't even there:

Dorm life can sometimes get a little bit dull and sometimes students like to prank one another. But 99.9% of the time the prank is funny to the prankster and not to the prankee. When I first moved into the dorms I was walking through a neighboring suite to find two guys kneeling at the base of a dorm room door with a container of baby powder, a piece of paper, an extension cord and a blow dryer. I asked them what they were doing and they told me they had "pennied" a girl in her room. "Pennying" someone in the room consists of pushing inward on the bottom of the door with their foot to increase the gap between the door and the door frame and then taking a stack of pennies and slipping them into the gap, up towards the doorknob. When the pressure is released at the bottom of the door the pennies are firmly wedged in place, effectively putting so much pressure on the bolt that the person inside the room can't turn the doorknob. Now that they had the girl trapped in her room they proceeded to dump the baby powder onto the piece of paper, slip it under her door and turn on the blow dryer, creating a cloud of powder dust inside the girl's room. I thought they were a couple of dipsticks as they were chuckling to themselves like a couple of five year olds doing something naughty. I went on my way and it wasn't until the next day that I was approached by an R.A. (resident assistant) who asked me if I had been there when this prank took place. I said, "Well, I was walking by and saw them do it but I didn't know what they were doing at the time."

It seems that the girl didn't like being trapped in her room and decided to climb out the third floor window, where she fell and broke her arm. Since I was "there" I had a strike against me and was told that any further misconduct would lead to my being kicked out of the dorms.

That day I decided that if anything similar ever occurred I would deny having been there. Sure enough a month or two later there was an unauthorized party and the students involved where rounded up, and their names taken. When, a month later, the paperwork made its way to the housing office and I was called in to be disciplined. The housing office worker lady asked me what I had to say for myself and I said, "I wasn't even there."

Her brows shot up and she asked, "You weren't there?"

I said, "No. I go home for the weekends." I told her, "I don't know how they would have gotten my name." I was told that I could go and no further action was taken.

If somebody has pictures, I was always told to say, "That's not me. Yeah, It sorta looks like me but, like I said, I wasn't even there."

Go to the emergency room:

If you find yourself the victim of a prank or plural pranks there are easy ways to stop people pranking you. Let's say someone puts clear plastic wrap across the opening of your door so that when you walk out it causes you to smash your face and fall on your back. If you hold your neck and groan and moan or even go to the emergency room it's pretty obvious that you won't be pranked again. Chances are someone was videotaping it on a cell phone. That could get you a hefty settlement.

If you feel like being a prankster remember that every time you do a prank you're spinning the wheel. Things could go horribly wrong and you could find yourself not only expelled but at the end of a hefty lawsuit. If you're a guy remember that girls don't dig pranksters.

There are several pranks one should watch out for in

college. The plastic wrap over the toilet is one. Never take candy from a stranger is a good saying since, unfortunately, people still try to pass off laxatives as candy. People getting woken up by being hit by a ball or something else is another prank that really ticks me off. Telling people you have a herniated disc in your neck might deter them from such action. I knew one guy who took a baseball bat and went to town on a pranksters dorm room door knob. The kid had to wait two days for a new door knob before he could get in his room.

When to keep your mouth shut:
If you have ever watched a real life cop show on TV you've seen a criminal seated in a little interrogation room being grilled by detectives. The crook who talks goes to jail. If someone's putting pressure on you whether to talk or to buy a car tell them you need to use the bathroom to get some time to collect yourself. If you're under 18 the only thing out of your mouth to the cops should be, "I want my mom and dad." If you're over 18 the only words out of your mouth should be, "I want a lawyer."

What might seem to you like a bit of fun might be seen differently by the police and might cost you not only money, it might cost you your reputation and your liberty. Never believe it when someone tells you, "You won't be in any trouble. Just tell us what happened."

There are cops and then there are cops. Some of the best people I've known have been cops, as are some of the worst.

Don't take the rap:
Don't take the rap for someone else. Examples are: switching seats with a drunk driver so they won't get in trouble, taking drugs from someone who has a prior conviction. It's called being a conspirator and could land you in jail. It happens all the time and usually in the excitement of the moment. Decide ahead of time not to

take the rap for a friend. If your friend couldn't do the time they shouldn't have done the crime.

Chapter 5
Never Put It In Writing

Never write it down. If you have beef with someone or want to say something negative there is an old mafia adage that says: never put things in writing when you can say it and never say it when you can indicate something with a gesture.

Every thing you write can be used against you:
Emails and texts can be used in evidence against you, as can social media. Everyone has a camera in his or her cell phone so keep that in the back of your mind when you've had a few drinks and feel like being a crazy person. If you ever find a picture of yourself on a social media site doing something you're embarrassed of you might want to threaten the person responsible with legal action (or worse, and never in writing) unless they want to take it down. If you do feel like getting "crazy" it might be better to do so in the privacy of your own room. Many, many reputations and dignities have been shattered by one or two seconds of recklessness in, say, exposing body parts that shouldn't be exposed in public just to have them sent from cell phone to cell phone like wildfire. If you make a decision not to do certain things before consuming alcohol the brain will retain that after you've consumed alcohol.

Chapter 6
The First Two Weeks

The first two weeks of school suck! Every year at the start of term, for the first two weeks, one can't help but walk by freshmen crying into their phones, "I want to come home!" The first two weeks of school or in a new job or anything different can be rough. Being given piles of homework by professors, trying to find classes, getting used to be cheap cafeteria food, the smell of a new roommate and being away from home can be overwhelming. This is natural. Once you're able to start juggling your homework things get a great deal better. If you go in realizing that the first two weeks can be somewhat nightmarish it makes it a lot easier to deal with.

Chapter 7
Use Legal Terms

Use legal words. To get a problem was something changed before you go to whoever it is can make that change you have to do several things: put yourself in their position and think what argument can I use that they cannot refuse. If your roommate smells bad it doesn't take showers doesn't wash the clothes what can you say to the head of housing? The head of housing you ask? Shouldn't I go to a resident assistant first? A resident assistant is a student who gets free room and board in exchange for policing their other students. Some of them are cool some of them are power-hungry sharks. Their mantra is, "Let's see how things go." So when you go to the head of housing do you just say, "My roommate stinks. I want another room"?

No. You say my roommate is so odiferous it's giving me hives. It's affecting my breathing. Get a note from your family doctor. Tell them how bad your roommate smells and that it's causing you lack of sleep, making you nauseous and giving you an acid stomach. Ask your doctor for a note to have your room moved. Housing isn't going to want to go against your doctor's orders. You are far more likely to get a new room assignment with a doctor's note in hand.

Nobody wants to be sued:
If someone is giving you a hard time and you need to tell somebody about it use words like "harassment" or "hazing". Schools don't want that publicity. If you use legal words like harassment or hazing that is something they will take seriously, very much more so if you put it in writing. In any situation like this keep records of times when you talk to people, what was said and any emails of course. If someone gives you an answer that you don't like ask them

to put it in writing. They'll think twice about giving you a negative response in writing that might be shown around and talked about. This works not only in college but also in the workplace. Nobody wants to be sued so use legal terms. Don't be too brazen about it. Be cool, not overtly threatening. It's always more important to get what you want rather than to be "right". If someone is doing you wrong give them an opportunity to save face by making things right.

If you want to threaten somebody never threaten them outright. Say something like, "It would be unfortunate if that were to happen…" or "If this continues I may be forced to take steps…" Threatening someone nowadays is a criminal offense. If you should ever say anything in the heat of the moment deny everything. "You must have misheard me. I would never say anything like that."

Chapter 8
Self Defense

Stab them with a pen:
If you have to walk in a dark parking lot at night people say to put your keys between your fingers as a weapon. That's ridiculous. Nothing beats a good ballpoint pen for penetration. An attacker will call it quits quickly if you stab them hard, fast and repeatedly in the face, chest or pretty much anywhere with a ball point pen.

I know a very nice, very pretty girl who, incidentally, is a ballet dancer who one night went across the hall to hang out with "the guys". The guys had been drinking heavily and one of them got it in his head that he could do whatever he wanted. He pinned this girl against the wall. She struggled and said, "Let me go" repeatedly to no avail. The other guys in the room did nothing. Having had self-defense training, she decked him in the chest with her palms, sending him flat on his back. Only then did the other guys get up to help. Her attacker was later expelled, not for attacking her but for the next girl he attacked. Self-defense classes are free and there are lots of videos on the Internet. Knowing a few moves could save your life. If you don't have time to take a self-defense class just know that striking someone hard and repeatedly in the throat will usually make them let you go.

Self-defense classes don't teach you to stab with a pen. I guess it sounds barbaric. I'm talking about life threatening situations here. Stabbing someone in the throat may seem barbaric but getting attacked or sexually assaulted is pretty damn barbaric too.

In the old days sexual predators wouldn't last five minutes in prison. The prisoners would take care of them while the guards looked the other way. Sexual criminals weren't treated too gently by the cops back then either.

Not all attacks are physical. Psychological abuse is, in my opinion, many ways worse than physical abuse. Stick up for yourself from the get go. Use terms like: harassment, bite me, or act bored with them and say, "What ever." You can also invite your favorite Uncle for a visit.

When one of my nephews was 14 and hanging out with his friends I told them that if anyone tried to get him to do drugs I'd break their legs. One of my nephew's friends said, "You'd go to jail."

I told him, "You think so? I'd tell the judge they were trying to get my nephew to do drugs. What do you think the judge would say?" To tell you the truth, I have no idea what a judge would say, but I'm pretty sure none of my nephew's friends was in a hurry to get him to try drugs.

Chapter 9
Theft & Trust

Trust no one:

There are a lot of scammers; liars and thieves in the world so don't wear your heart on your sleeve. People will respect you if you say no. No, I never lend money. No, I can't give you a ride home. Just because you have a car doesn't mean you're a taxi service. Never, ever loan your schoolbooks to anyone. Never loan your building key to anyone and never let someone in who doesn't belong. You don't want it on your conscience if they should do something heinous. I remember one time when group of local twenty-somethings walked through the dorms through propped open doors and stole pocketbooks from open rooms. A group of students who were building a loft (a fancy name for a framework to raise a bed off the floor to slip a desk under it) saw the thieves and chased them out of the dorms with two by fours they had been building with. The police caught them.

Watch your stuff:

I remember another time when someone stole a book bag from the pile next to the doors in the campus arcade. A student saw him and he was caught and expelled. He had planned on selling the books at the school bookstore as used. Keep your book bag with you and if you're playing a videogame stand on one of the straps.

Don't tempt thieves:

It's pretty rotten for student to steal from his fellow students but it happens all the time. One guy was stealing radios out of student's cars in the dorm parking lot until he was caught and expelled. My friend Jack had a CD collection on his front seat that I noticed as we were walking into the dorms. I told him that would be tempting to a thief but he wasn't worried. The next morning his car window was broken and his CDs were gone.

Chapter 10
Don't Get It In Your Name

Don't get it in your name. When I lived off campus all of the bills were put in my roommates name: electrical, fuel oil, telephone and cable. I told them that my credit was bad which was a falsehood. I was not comfortable having my name on an account where I would be collecting money from my roommates. Sure enough there were problems. The electricity was shut off as well as the phone. One of the roommates had been collecting the money and using it to buy drugs. If you don't have to sign your name, don't.

Chapter 11
On Locals

Every college town or every area around the college people are known as "locals." Locals aren't typically very fond of college students, who they see as noisy, privileged troublemakers. No, the locals aren't fond of college students and neither are the local police. For this reason I like to have my car serviced at home rather than at school.

Chapter 12
Diarrhea

Diarrhea is a wonderful word and can get you out of many sticky situations. I was late for class one day, having been detained by a teacher, and when I walked in late to my class the teacher said, "You're late. Leave." On the spur of the moment I blurted out, "I have diarrhea."

Perhaps he felt embarrassed by making me say that in front of all the other students but he said, "Oh, um, you can stay."

If you find yourself cornered some night by a creep or a girl craving your attention and you would rather chew off your own arm than spend another minute with them you can say, "I have diarrhea." If you get pulled over for speeding and the cop asks why you were going so fast, you could say, "I have diarrhea." The possibilities are endless.

Chapter 13
How Students Die

The table on the balcony:
Every year some student gets the bright idea of putting their kitchen table out on the balcony, where someone invariably has to put one of the kitchen chairs on top of the table and sit in it. Every year one of these people goes head over heels dies.

Out the window:
Another common way for a college student to die is to sit on one of the wall-mounted heaters and lean back against the open window, falling several stories onto the concrete. Seriously, a little bar riveted across the window would save a lot of lives, but since they don't do that please don't lean against the open window.

Steroid use:
Steroid use is another way college students die.

Suicide:
I was pretty close friends with this one group of girls and one of their members ended up taking their own life with a mixture of antidepressants and alcohol. Many people suffer from depression and take medication to help control it. This is nothing for people to be ashamed of nothing that should be a subject for Taboo. However, there are many medications that set on the labels not to mix them with alcohol. If you take one of these medications, or have a friend that does, drinking should be pretty big NO. If you have an inkling that someone is contemplating suicide TELL SOMEONE. You don't want to live with guilt if you don't. People are so worried about being a rat. If you are, make an anonymous call or two or three…

Peer pressure kills:

Peer pressure can be pretty strong especially where drinking is concerned. Make the decision ahead of time not to drink if you're taking a prescription medication that forbids it. Also make the decision ahead of time not to get into a car with someone who's for the driver that has been or will be drinking. Adding a lime to a glass of Coke or soda water will disguise your drink so that nobody will put pressure on you to drink.

I knew of a kid whose friends dared him to spray lock deicer on his tongue. His tongue swelled up and he choked to death on it.

Drunk Driving:

Never get in a car with someone who's been drinking.

Sliding off the hood:

Every year somebody has to take a ride on the hood, roof or trunk of a car. Invariably they slide off and either end up under a tire or wrapped around a pole.

Chapter 14
On Fighting

Fighting is a big no in school. If one of your friends picks a fight with someone, let them have at it. If people ask why you don't jump then say something like, "I only fight when I get paid to fight." That will get them.

"You messing with my sister?":

If some dude is giving a girl a hard time and you feel that you have to stick up for her try this line, "Dude, are you giving my sister a hard time?" Sisters are sacred, and no one will pick a fight with you for sticking up for your sister. I've used it and it works great. Of course the girl always rolls her eyes at me afterwards and asks, "I'm your sister now?" And I just say, "It worked, didn't it?" Another line to avoid a fight is, "I just got out of the hospital but if you want to wait a week…" Or gee, do I want to fight? I just got out of prison so…"

I don't go for the macho crap:

Tell your girlfriend up front that you don't go for all that macho crap. Tell her that if some stranger says something inappropriate to her, you'd rather you and she leave than have you get stabbed by a stranger. If she's not cool with that, maybe she's not for you. Scumbags will think nothing of stabbing someone, especially squirrely, undernourished, scumbags. There was a man who got into a fight over a washing machine in a laundromat and stabbed another man to death. When asked if he would do it again he said, "Yes."

There are ways to fight without fighting. "Accidentally" elbowing someone in the face is one. The trick is to look like a wimp when doing it in case you're on camera.

Defending yourself and fighting are two different things. If someone attacks you and you can't run, destroy them.

The cops!:

If you see two strangers fighting it's not smart to jump in. Yell, "The cops!" and point around the corner to make the fighters believe the cops are coming. They'll take off.

Chapter 15
On Parties

This goes for guys and girls:
Never accept a drink from anyone and never leave your drink unattended. If someone asks for your number and you don't want to give it say NO or, "Sorry, I never give that out." Don't put your personal info, address, phone number etc., online. Don't leave a party with a stranger. Just because you go to the same school doesn't make somebody trustworthy, and non-students crash parties all the time. If someone insists on driving or walking you home or to your room it's OK to refuse.

If you feel uncomfortable or the hairs on the back of your neck stand on end use the old saying: When in doubt, get the heck out. Don't be afraid of looking "uncool" by saying no to anything you don't want to do. There is no one more important than you. Just because someone is an authority figure: campus police, resident assistant, teacher etc, nobody has the right to make you do something that you know is wrong.

$20:
Have money for a cab in case your ride bails.

Fighting is fun but not for school:
Don't hang out with creeps, slimeballs or wierdos. If a party is crashed by a group of creeps ask them to leave. If they decline, pretend to call the police. If they still don't leave, call the police. Don't expect the police to be nice. When I lived off campus I called the cops on a group of party crashers and the cops were not nice. The guys left though. Could I have fought them? Yes. Would it have been fun? Yes. Would I have been breaking my rule of not fighting in school? Yes. Would I ever tell anyone about my

rule for not fighting in school? No. A snake doesn't have to bite when he can show his teeth.

Control:
When I lived off campus we had a pretty big party. The alcohol consumption and ticket sales was controlled, the guy / girl ratio was 50 / 50 (I sold tickets to the girls. The guys were too shy) and it was great. I made $700 that night.

Incognito:
Adding a lime to a glass of Coke or soda water will disguise your drink so that nobody will put pressure on you to drink.

I just puked:
If a guy or girl is hitting on you and you want nothing to do with them try saying, "I just puked."

Have $20 in your pocket at all times in case you need a cab. Yeah, I already said that. It's important.

Have emergency numbers written down in your wallet in case your phone dies or you lose it.

Nobody left behind:
Travel in a pack with the understanding "Nobody left behind." This includes your friend who should be voted most likely to get crabs in college.

I once drove several girls to the store. It was around noon and we were just leaving the store when a van full of local guys pulled up and asked the girls if they wanted to go to a party. The guys were ratty looking and I didn't figure there was any party on a weekday at noontime. The girls smiled and told the locals, "OK!"

I shook my head and said, "Come on, I'm taking you back to the dorms."

One of the locals looked pretty mad and said, "They're coming with us."

I ignored the dude and told the girls, "I'm not going to be the one to tell your mothers that I was the last person to see you alive. I drove you to the store and I'm driving you back. If you want to go to a party after that, fine."

The girls got in my car and I drove them back to the dorms.

Thinking back on it, I used the same tone with those girls I would use with my little sister when she was about to do something stupid. If that sounds chauvinistic I can only say that I've stood up for guys as well, sometimes stupidly. Don't be afraid to call the campus cops or shout for the guys next door if you need help.

Don't buy for minors:

Don't buy alcohol for minors no matter how attractive they are. Tell them you've already been busted once for buying for minors and you don't want it to happen again. If somebody wraps himself around a tree you don't want to be responsible.

Chapter 16
Get It In Writing

Get it in writing:
A person should always keep a receipt even if it's just for a stick of gum. It might afford you a valuable alibi should the need arise.

My brother transferred colleges and was told that his new school would accept so many of his credits. Since our Mother drilled the need for us to get things down in writing, my brother asked the person who told him that his credits were accepted to write him a note to that effect. My brother was told, "Don't worry about it." But my brother was insistent and got his note with the signature of the head of the Education Department. When it came time to graduate my brother was told that he was nine credits shy of graduation and that not all of his course credits had been transferred. My brother was in shock until he remembered that he had that note. He ran back to his off-campus house as fast as he could and rummaged through drawers and boxes until he found it. Returning to the head of the Education Department a short time later he presented him with the note and was told that he would graduate.

Chapter 17
Stuff to Bring To School

Stuff to bring to school that you don't find on the average list:
An external hard drive with automatic backup capability. A couple of USB zip drives are cool too. Having a computer without having a backup is like being on the Titanic without a lifeboat. If you can't figure out the automatic back up, have someone who knows how to do it for you and do it BEFORE you need it. Also have either system restore software on a disc or on a USB drive. You know that if your computer decides to fail it will do so when you need it the most.

Bring the tacky stuff that you can put pictures up on your walls without taking off the paint. I knew students who accidentally made holes in their walls and filled them with toothpaste so they weren't charged for them.

Bring flip-flops for the shower so you don't get athletes foot.

Athlete's foot spray or powder for when you do get athletes foot.

The little colored tabs for notebooks that you stick to the edges of the pages are great for textbooks enabling you to quickly find chapters that you're looking for.

Not only sluts carry condoms:
If you are sexually active... Wait... If you have gone through puberty then for heavens sake, have a supply of condoms!
I knew this one girl from the dorms who was really cute. She was a petite blonde with a great smile and sparkling

blue eyes. They had a school dance and I asked her to go. I wondered at the time why she looked so distraught when I asked her. She told me no, and I was more than a little bummed out. I found out later that she was pregnant when I asked her (I'm guessing a boy from her home town), and had quit school a week later. I like to think that she would have wanted to go with me. I still wonder how she is doing long after graduation.

Some people might think, "Oh, if I have condoms and my mother finds them she'll think I'm a slut." (I've known several male sluts. I believe they run 50/50) Would you rather explain to your mother how you're being responsible or would you rather give her a talk about how you or your girlfriend is pregnant? Nobody plans to get a flat tire but you carry a spare right?

Locker stuff:
A combination lock for the gym locker. Extra shampoo, soap, swimsuit, deodorant, t-shirt and towel for locker.

Chapter 18
On Cheating

A crime not worth the time:

Criminals will tell you that there are crimes not worth doing. Robbing a bank is one of them. You get the longest sentence (the most time) for the lowest payoff. Cheating is like robbing a bank. The rewards don't merit the risk.

On cheating. Don't do it! If you cheat not only will you be expelled, you'll find it very difficult to get into any college. Even if you don't get caught you won't have any pride whatsoever in your education and will treat your diploma like a soiled rag. You'll end up feeling like a big-time loser. If you have a class that the only way you can pass is by cheating, then withdraw from the class and take it during the summer with a cool teacher.

Don't let anyone cheat off your paper; it can get you expelled. If you see someone trying to cheat off you, raise your hand and ask for another seat. If, afterwards, the cheater gets mad and says, "What the hell!" you get madder and say, "You could have gotten me expelled, you fricken idiot!" Take the moral high ground. An old mafia adage is: It's business, not personal.

Chapter 19
Meeting People

Tigers go solo when looking for a mate:

When my suitemates saw that many people would wave and say hello to me they would ask, "How do you know so many people?" Or, "How do you know so many girls?" My invariable response was, "Because I don't hang out with you guys all the time."

Once, I was sitting at my desk and my suitemates came into my room like a like a gaggle of geese, all shoulder to shoulder, and asked, "Are you coming to dinner with us?"

They looked so comical that I said, "What, do you want me to hold your hand? I'll see you at the cafeteria." I like my alone time and I found that one of the best ways to meet people is in the cafeteria. I would get my lunch, breakfast, or dinner tray, walk to a table with one or more girls that I thought I might like to meet and simply ask, "Do you mind if I sit here?"

I can't remember ever having been turned away. It wasn't a very large percentage of new people I would meet that I would like to spend more time with but I did meet a lot of nice, interesting people. Some of the girls I would meet were so extraordinarily beautiful that they would have very few friends. I think that people were put off by how attractive they were. If you want to meet people and have some cool relationships, be yourself. Don't gossip and don't treat girls like they're some other species. Girls aren't unicorns! They have the same emotions guys do.

Ask them out:

If you want to ask someone out, ask! If you don't you'll kick yourself when, years later, you hear the words, "I had such a crush on you!"

Guys can be dense:

Girls, if I learned one thing in college it's that guys can be pretty dense. A girl asked me to go to an astronomy thing one night and I replied, "Thanks, but I'm not into astronomy." I didn't get it that she was asking me out on a date. If she had asked me out for a pizza it would have been a different story.

Off campus:

If you live off campus meeting people can be a bit more difficult. Fortunately there are sports, the gym and campus cafeterias to make new acquaintances in. Don't be shy in asking, "What's going on this weekend?" and "Where are the parties this weekend?" If a group of people isn't to your taste move on.

Chapter 20
Getting Good Grades

PREEMPTIVE STRIKE:
Take everything on your syllabuses and put it in the calendar of your planner. This way you'll know ahead of time if you have three papers due at the same time and do them ahead of time so you won't be swamped.

SKIP THE REMEDIAL:
Take any optional placement tests you can! They're free. Competitive colleges will waive courses for which you have a proficiency, enabling you to take other classes you need instead.

FOUR COLOR PEN:
Take notes in black and or blue. Any questions you have write in green. After each class ask the teacher your questions. This is known as "filling the holes in your knowledge." Important points put in red ink. This makes it easier to study.

People who take notes on a laptop have poorer retention / results than those who hand write their notes.

Take practice tests online from other universities.

If you have a huge assignment midway through the semester start working on it early and do a little each day.

Chapter 21
Making Extra Money

FREE LAUNDRY:
You have to stay and watch your own laundry so why not tell a friend that you'll do their laundry as well in exchange for the quarters for your own machines?

There are always coins behind the soda machine. I don't think I paid for a single vending machine drink in college.

Babysitting is easy:
Sign up for babysitting through Student Services. It's good cash and parents will pick you up and drop you off.

Volunteer:
Volunteer at the campus bookstore. You'll have first pick at used books so you'll get one that's up to date and pretty fresh. You'll also get a hefty discount.

Volunteers often get great perks: Free trips, food, meeting people…

Campus meal plan too expensive? Sign up for weekdays and stock up on fruit and cereal for the weekends.

Chapter 22
Other Stuff

Dorm beds can be pretty cheap. I had one that had a wire mesh with springs attached to a metal frame. I sank down about the foot when I would lie on it. A piece of plywood between the frame and the mattress can do wonders.

If your school has a pool be sure to pick up a pair of swinging swimming goggles as college pool chlorine levels can reach Chernobyl levels.

Take advantage of the gym.

There are many cool clubs that go on trips all over the place for short money.

When going out to a restaurant always make sure to say you'll pay for your own meal. Why pay for someone else's lobster when you're having a salad.

When I was in college I was always hungry. One neat trick I learned was that if someone wanted me to, say, help them move their belongings from one place to another I would ask, "Is there a pizza in it for me?" I ate a lot of pizza.

Everybody likes pizza. If you want to ask someone out for dinner, don't. Ask them if they want to get a pizza. It sounds much more carefree and fun then going out to "dinner".

Take a permanent marker and put your initials on the white cotton inside pocket of your jeans to prevent mix ups and theft.

Bring stuff home on your Christmas holiday that you found you didn't need.

College is a hotbed for atheism. Don't apologize for your religion or beliefs. You don't have to argue the validity of your religion. You don't owe that to anyone.

Don't leave your razor out. If somebody "missed a spot" and grabs your razor you could get HIV.

Never leave your toothbrush out! Have a spare toothbrush or two.

Lysol everything. Mom's not there to clean the bathroom so a quick spray with Lysol could save you from the nasty.

College students don't plan on getting sick. Know where to go before you get sick or hurt. Medical insurance for students can be really inexpensive when bought through the school. I knew a young guy who (I would think it illegal) would sign up for a class each year to get his medical insurance, then withdraw two days later, getting his money for the class back but keeping the medical insurance.

Don't forget to have fun in college.

People change careers an average of seven times in the course of their lives in the U.S. Take a major that floats your boat, not to impress other people.

About the Author

Antonio Rossini was born the fourth of six children. Antonio Rossini holds a Bachelor of Science in electrical engineering.

Acknowledgments

I would like to express my gratitude to all the people who encouraged me in the writing of this guide. Many, many thanks to my Mother, my sister Maia and my four brothers: Ted, David, Jonathan and Christopher for their generous inspiration. Thanks to Angelo, Jonny, Leah, Laura, Christopher, Austin, Zach, Emily, Graeme, Ani, Zack, Kate and Jack. Special thanks to the select group of horrible roommates and teachers that inspired me to write this guide; may you get what you have given.

Made in the USA
Middletown, DE
04 June 2017